Made in United States
Orlando, FL
28 January 2022

14173879R00074